COMPILED BY
CHARLOTTE AND WOLF LESLAU
AND WITH
DECORATIONS BY JEFF HILL

PETER PAUPER PRESS, INC.
WHITE PLAINS • NEW YORK

ĀFRICAN PROVERBS

■ ■ ■

PROVERBS ON PROVERBS

■ ■ ■

Proverbs are the daughters of experience.
(Sierra Leone)

■ ■ ■

A proverb is the horse of conversation:
when the conversation lags, a
proverb will revive it.
(Yoruba)

■ ■ ■

A wise man who knows proverbs,
reconciles difficulties.
(Yoruba)

Rain beats a leopard's skin, but it does not wash out the spots.

■   ■   ■

Wood already touched by fire is not hard to set alight.

■   ■   ■

It is the wife who knows her husband.

■   ■   ■

Only when you have crossed the river, can you say the crocodile has a lump on his snout.

■   ■   ■

If you are in hiding, don't light a fire.

■   ■   ■

One falsehood spoils a thousand truths.

When a man is wealthy, he may wear an old cloth.

■　■　■

Do not call the forest that shelters you a jungle.

■　■　■

Hunger is felt by a slave and hunger is felt by a king.

■　■　■

The moon moves slowly, but it crosses the town.

■　■　■

The ruin of a nation begins in the homes of its people.

■　■　■

When the cock is drunk, he forgets about the hawk.

■　■　■

There is no medicine to cure hatred.

■　■　■

It's a bad child who does not take advice.

8

When a man is coming toward you, you need not say: "Come here."

■ ■ ■

Even though the old man is strong and hearty, he will not live forever.

■ ■ ■

When a king has good counselors, his reign is peaceful.

■ ■ ■

By the time the fool has learned the game, the players have dispersed.

■ ■ ■

The poor man and the rich man do not play together.

■ ■ ■

It is the calm and silent water that drowns a man.

■ ■ ■

When you follow in the path of your father, you learn to walk like him.

When a woman is hungry, she says, "Roast something for the children that they may eat."

■   ■   ■

What is bad luck for one man is good luck for another.

■   ■   ■

When the fool is told a proverb, its meaning has to be explained to him.

■   ■   ■

He who cannot dance will say: "The drum is bad."

■   ■   ■

One cannot both feast and become rich.

■   ■   ■

It is no shame at all to work for money.

■   ■   ■

Money is sharper than a sword.

■   ■   ■

It is the fool's sheep that break loose twice.

When you are rich, you are hated; when you are poor, you are despised.

■ ■ ■

It is Mr. Old-Man-Monkey who marries Mrs. Old-Woman-Monkey.

■ ■ ■

Fire and gunpowder do not sleep together.

■ ■ ■

No one tests the depth of a river with both feet.

■ ■ ■

Two small antelopes can beat a big one.

Do not try to cook the goat's young in the goat's milk.

The humble pay for the mistakes of their betters.

■ ■ ■

You are beautiful because of your possessions.

■ ■ ■

A man with too much ambition cannot sleep in peace.

It is best to bind up the finger before it is cut.

■ ■ ■

If the palm of the hand itches, it signifies the coming of great luck.

■ ■ ■

Sickness accompanies a waning moon; a new moon cures disease.

When the moon is not full, the stars shine more brightly.

■ ■ ■

He who hunts two rats, catches none.

■ ■ ■

If you burn a house, can you conceal the smoke?

■ ■ ■

A strawberry blossom will not sweeten dry bread.

■ ■ ■

When the master is absent, the frogs hop into the house.

■ ■ ■

He who is bitten by a snake fears a lizard.

13

If you do not step on the dog's tail, he will not bite you.

■   ■   ■

When the vine entwines your roof, it is time to cut it down.

■   ■   ■

He who asks questions, cannot avoid the answers.

■   ■   ■

The flood takes him in, and the ebb takes him out.

■   ■   ■

She is like a road — pretty, but crooked.

14

By trying often, the monkey learns to jump from the tree.

■   ■   ■

The heart of the wise man lies quiet like limpid water.

■   ■   ■

The cricket cries, the year changes.

■   ■   ■

Thought breaks the heart.

■   ■   ■

Knowledge is better than riches.

■   ■   ■

Rain does not fall on one roof alone.

■   ■   ■

An elephant will reach to the roof of the house.

■   ■   ■

A man's wealth may be superior to him.

Lower your head modestly while passing, and you will harvest bananas.

■   ■   ■

What is said over the dead lion's body, could not be said to him alive.

■   ■   ■

Children are the reward of life.

■   ■   ■

Being well dressed does not prevent one from being poor.

■   ■   ■

Little by little grow the bananas.

■   ■   ■

A pretty basket does not prevent worries.

No matter how full the river, it still wants to grow.

■ ■ ■

Do not dispose of the monkey's tail before he is dead.

■ ■ ■

Love is like a baby: it needs to be treated tenderly.

■ ■ ■

The teeth are smiling, but is the heart?

■ ■ ■

Great events may stem from words of no importance.

■ ■ ■

You do not teach the paths of the forest to an old gorilla.

■ ■ ■

A little subtleness is better than a lot of force.

■ ■ ■

Two birds disputed about a kernel, when a third swooped down and carried it off.

17

The son shoots a leopard; the father is proud.

■ ■ ■

Man is like palm-wine: when young, sweet but without strength; in old age, strong but harsh.

■ ■ ■

Mothers-in-law are hard of hearing.

■ ■ ■

If you tell people to live together, you tell them to quarrel.

■ ■ ■

The friends of our friends are our friends.

■ ■ ■

Wood may remain ten years in the water, but it will never become a crocodile.

■ ■ ■

Death does not sound a trumpet.

■ ■ ■

Let him speak who has seen with his eyes.

8 195,00 ✗
11. 876.00

13,896
_____

162.   ROBERT
 25   M^c GEE
 21
,42   621 4113
17 1
 25

When the bee comes to your house, let her have beer; you may want to visit the bee's house some day.

■　■　■

No matter how long the night, the day is sure to come.

■　■　■

He who is free of faults, will never die.

■　■　■

A single bracelet does not jingle.

■　■　■

To love someone who does not love you, is like shaking a tree to make the dew drops fall.

■　■　■

Sleep is the cousin of death.

■　■　■

The flesh of a young animal tastes flat.

■　■　■

Those who are absent are always wrong.

19

To one who does not know, a small garden is a forest.

■   ■   ■

When one is in love, a cliff becomes a meadow.

■   ■   ■

A fool looks for dung where the cow never browsed.

■   ■   ■

The cattle is as good as the pasture in which it grazes.

■   ■   ■

Evil enters like a needle and spreads like an oak tree.

■   ■   ■

A close friend can become a close enemy.

What is inflated too much, will burst into fragments.

■   ■   ■

Restless feet may walk into a snake pit.

■   ■   ■

A coward sweats in water.

■   ■   ■

Snake at your feet — a stick at your hand!

■   ■   ■

The witness of a rat is another rat.

■   ■   ■

He who learns, teaches.

■   ■   ■

A fool will pair an ox with an elephant.

■   ■   ■

One who runs alone cannot be outrun by another.

■   ■   ■

Cactus is bitter only to him who tastes of it.

21

The frog wanted to be as big as the elephant, and burst.

■   ■   ■

One who recovers from sickness, forgets about God.

■   ■   ■

Termites live underground.

■   ■   ■

Woman without man is like a field without seed.

■   ■   ■

If a friend hurts you, run to your wife.

■   ■   ■

If the heart is sad, tears will flow.

■   ■   ■

Unless you call out, who will open the door?

■   ■   ■

Her horns are not too heavy for the cow.

There is no one who became rich because he broke a holiday, and no one who became fat because he broke a fast.

■ ■ ■

When the heart overflows, it comes out through the mouth.

■ ■ ■

You cannot build a house for last year's summer.

■ ■ ■

A partner in the business will not put an obstacle to it.

■ ■ ■

When spider webs unite, they can tie up a lion.

■ ■ ■

He who digs too deep for a fish, may come out with a snake.

■ ■ ■

Confiding a secret to an unworthy person is like carrying grain in a bag with a hole.

23

A loose tooth will not rest until it's pulled out.

■　■　■

The dog I bought, bit me; the fire I kindled, burned me.

■　■　■

A blade won't cut another blade; a cheat won't cheat another cheat.

■　■　■

If one is not in a hurry, even an egg will start walking.

■　■　■

If relatives help each other, what evil can hurt them?

■　■　■

A home without a woman is like a barn without cattle.

■　■　■

Sitting is being crippled.

■　■　■

The fool speaks, the wise man listens.

24

A cat may go to a monastery, but she still remains a cat!

■　■　■

I have a cow in the sky, but cannot drink her milk.

■　■　■

Dine with a stranger but save your love for your family.

■　■　■

A too modest man goes hungry.

■　■　■

If you offend, ask for pardon; if offended, forgive.

■　■　■

He who conceals his disease cannot expect to be cured.

■　■　■

A fool and water will go the way they are diverted.

■　■　■

Where there is no shame, there is no honor.

A silly daughter teaches her mother how to bear children.

■   ■   ■

Advise and counsel him; if he does not listen, let adversity teach him.

■   ■   ■

Anticipate the good so that you may enjoy it.

■   ■   ■

Clothes put on while running come off while running.

■   ■   ■

A cow gave birth to a fire: she wanted to lick it, but it burned; she wanted to leave it, but she could not because it was her own child.

■   ▨   ■

One scoops with a scoop.

■   ■   ■

Living is worthless for one without a home.

26

When one sets a portion for oneself, usually it is not too small.

■   ■   ■

He who wants to barter, usually knows what is best for him.

■   ■   ■

She who does not yet know how to walk, cannot climb a ladder.

■   ■   ■

When a fool is cursed, he thinks he is being praised.

■   ■   ■

It is easy to become a monk in one's old age.

■   ■   ■

Singing "Halleluia" everywhere does not prove piety.

■   ■   ■

Saying that it's for her child, she gets herself a loaf of bread.

What has been blown away, cannot be found again.

■ ■ ■

The fool is thirsty in the midst of water.

■ ■ ■

Even over cold pudding, the coward says:
"It will burn my mouth."

■ ■ ■

What one hopes for is always better than what one has.

■ ■ ■

A single stick may smoke, but it will not burn.

■ ■ ■

As the wound inflames the finger, so thought inflames the mind.

He who lives with an ass, makes noises like an ass.

■   ■   ■

If a man comes, a quarrel comes.

■   ■   ■

Move your neck according to the music.

■   ■   ■

One is born, one dies; the land increases.

If there were no elephant in the jungle, the buffalo would be a great animal.

■   ■   ■

A crab does not beget a bird.

■   ■   ■

If you find no fish, you have to eat bread.

One camel does not make fun of the other camel's hump.

■ ■ ■

The man on his feet carries off the share of the man sitting down.

■ ■ ■

Around a flowering tree, one finds many insects.

■ ■ ■

To make preparations does not spoil the trip.

■ ■ ■

He who has done evil, expects evil.

■ ■ ■

A good deed is something one returns.

He who does not cultivate his field, will die of hunger.

■　■　■

A cow that has no tail should not try to chase away flies.

■　■　■

The toad likes water, but not when it's boiling.

■　■　■

Knowledge is like a garden : if it is not cultivated, it cannot be harvested.

■　■　■

When a needle falls into a deep well, many people will look into the well, but few will be ready to go down after it.

■　■　■

To have two eyes is cause for pride; but to have one eye is better than to have none.

Save your fowl before it stops flapping.

■   ■   ■

Too much discussion means a quarrel.

■   ■   ■

Mutual affection gives each his share.

■   ■   ■

Mutual gifts cement friendship.

■   ■   ■

It takes two to make a quarrel.

■   ■   ■

Two flavors confuse the palate.

■   ■   ■

He who talks incessantly, talks nonsense.

A little leaven smoothes away the whole lump.

■　■　■

Their mosquito won't bite me.

■　■　■

A bad son gives a bad name to his mother.

After a foolish deed comes remorse.

■　■　■

A man who has once been tossed by a buffalo, when he sees a black ox, thinks it's another buffalo.

■　■　■

He who receives a gift does not measure.

He who does not know one thing knows another.

■   ■   ■

Do not say the first thing that comes to your mind.

■   ■   ■

A white dog does not bite another white dog.

■   ■   ■

Try this bracelet: if it fits you wear it; but if it hurts you, throw it away no matter how shiny.

■   ■   ■

When you take a knife away from a child, give him a piece of wood instead.

■   ■   ■

He who is unable to dance says that the yard is stony.

■   ■   ■

One finger alone cannot kill even a louse.

34

Because a man has injured your goat, do not go out and kill his bull.

■ ■ ■

A man who continually laments is not heeded.

■ ■ ■

Talking with one another is loving one another.

■ ■ ■

Absence makes the heart forget.

■ ■ ■

If a dead tree falls, it carries with it a live one.

■ ■ ■

Virtue is better than wealth.

■ ■ ■

There is no phrase without a double meaning.

■ ■ ■

Hearts do not meet one another like roads.

One does not slaughter a calf before its mother's eyes.

■　■　■

There is no cure that does not cost.

■　■　■

Seeing is different from being told.

■　■　■

It is the duty of children to wait on elders, and not the elders on children.

■　■　■

Thunder is not yet rain.

■　■　■

Soon found soon lost.

■　■　■

Home affairs are not talked about on the public square.

■　■　■

Good millet is known at the harvest.

A little rain each day will fill the rivers to overflowing.

■ ■ ■

Do not measure the timbers for your house in the forest.

■ ■ ■

Though the palm tree in the jungle is big, who knows how big its yield will be?

Indecision is like the stepchild: if he doesn't wash his hands, he is called dirty; if he does, he is wasting the water.

The end of an ox is beef, and the end of a lie is grief.

■　■　■

Don't kick a sleeping dog.

■　■　■

Don't be so much in love that you can't tell when the rain comes.

■　■　■

Sorrow is like a precious treasure, shown only to friends.

■　■　■

Love is like young rice : transplanted, still it grows.

■　■　■

An eel that was not caught is as big as your thigh.

■　■　■

The dog's bark is not might, but fright.

■　■　■

Marriage is not a fast knot, but a slip knot.

38

Life is a shadow and a mist; it passes quickly by, and is no more.

■ ■ ■

Don't take another mouthful before you have swallowed what is in your mouth.

■ ■ ■

Cross the river in a crowd and the crocodile won't eat you.

■ ■ ■

Let your love be like the misty rain, coming softly, but flooding the river.

■ ■ ■

If you try to cleanse others — like soap, you will waste away in the process!

It is only the water that is spilt; the calabash is not broken!

He who wears too fine clothes, shall go about in rags.

■　■　■

Before eating, open thy mouth.

■　■　■

Too large a morsel chokes the child.

■　■　■

One must talk little, and listen much.

■　■　■

Not all the flowers of a tree produce fruit.

■　■　■

Two eyes see better than one.

■　■　■

He who loves money must labor.

■　■　■

If you watch your pot, your food will not burn.

■　■　■

Before one cooks, one must have the meat.

A cutting word is worse than a bowstring;
a cut may heal, but the cut of the tongue
does not.

■ ■ ■

He who begins a conversation, does not
foresee the end.

A proverb is the horse of conversation:
when the conversation lags, a proverb re-
vives it.

■ ■ ■

A wise man who knows his proverbs can
reconcile difficulties.

■ ■ ■

He who marries a beauty marries trouble.

Ashes fly back into the face of him who throws them.

■ ■ ■

He who does not mend his clothes will soon have none.

■ ■ ■

There is no medicine against old age.

■ ■ ■

He who boasts much can do little.

■ ■ ■

You cannot shave a man's head in his absence.

■ ■ ■

The egg becomes a cock.

■ ■ ■

Familiarity breeds contempt; distance breeds respect.

■ ■ ■

The rat cannot call the cat to account.

42

He who wishes to barter, does not like his own property.

■ ■ ■

Seeing is better than hearing.

■ ■ ■

Evil knows where evil sleeps.

■ ■ ■

He who is sick will not refuse medicine.

■ ■ ■

A wealthy man will always have followers.

■ ■ ■

The dying man is not saved by medicine.

■ ■ ■

Some birds avoid the water, ducks seek it.

43

The day on which one starts out is not the time to start one's preparations.

■　■　■

The house roof fights the rain, but he who is sheltered ignores it.

■　■　■

Since he has no eyes, he says that eyes smell bad.

■　■　■

He who is being carried does not realize how far the town is.

■　■　■

He who runs from the white ant may stumble upon the stinging ant.

■　■　■

The stone in the water does not know how hot the hill is, parched by the sun.

■　■　■

The one-eyed man thanks God only when he sees a man who is totally blind.

Someone else's legs do you no good in traveling.

■ ■ ■

Fine words do not produce food.

■ ■ ■

If the bull would throw you, lie down.

■ ■ ■

The bird flies high, but always returns to earth.

■ ■ ■

If you rise too early, the dew will wet you.

■ ■ ■

When the mouse laughs at the cat, there is a hole nearby.

■ ■ ■

Children of the same mother do not always agree.

■ ■ ■

What the child says, he has heard at home.

If you fill your mouth with a razor, you will spit blood.

■ ■ ■

Not to know is bad; not to wish to know is worse.

■ ■ ■

Before shooting, one must aim.

■ ■ ■

He who has goods can sell them.

■ ■ ■

When one is in trouble, one remembers God.

■ ■ ■

Meat does not eat meat.

■ ■ ■

Before healing others, heal thyself.

■ ■ ■

A shepherd does not strike his sheep.

A bird can drink much, but an elephant drinks more.

■ ■ ■

Horns do not grow before the head.

■ ■ ■

If the stomach-ache were in the foot, one would go lame.

■ ■ ■

Time destroys all things.

■ ■ ■

Earth is the queen of beds.

■ ■ ■

Little is better than nothing.

One little arrow does not kill a serpent.

Do not be like the mosquito that bites the owner of the house.

■ ■ ■

Wisdom is like mushrooms that come after you have finished eating (too late!).

If your mouth turns into a knife, it will cut off your lips.

■ ■ ■

A borrowed fiddle does not finish a tune.

■ ■ ■

The monkey does not see his own hind parts; he sees his neighbors'.

When the leopard is away, his cubs are eaten.

■   ■   ■

In a court of fowls, the cockroach never wins his case.

■   ■   ■

If you are building a house and a nail breaks, do you stop building, or do you change the nail?

■   ■   ■

Proverbs are the daughters of experience.

■   ■   ■

You set the trap after the rat has passed.

Spilled water is better than a broken jar.

■ ■ ■

Nobody tells all he knows.

■ ■ ■

The cow steps on the calf, but she does not hate it.

■ ■ ■

It is better to travel alone than with a bad companion.

■ ■ ■

Three kinds of people die poor: those who divorce, those who incur debts, and those who move around too much.

■ ■ ■

The heart is not a knee that can be bent.

If you speak, speak to him who understands you.

■   ■   ■

He may say that he loves you. Wait and see what he does for you!

■   ■   ■

The opportunity that God sends does not wake up him who is asleep.

■   ■   ■

To spend the night in anger is better than to spend it in repentance.

■   ■   ■

When you know who his friend is, you know who he is.

■   ■   ■

The truth is like gold: keep it locked up and you will find it exactly as you first put it away.

■   ■   ■

A healthy ear can stand hearing sick words.

51

If a centipede loses a leg, it does not prevent him from walking.

■　■　■

If your son laughs when you scold him, you ought to cry, for you have lost him; if he cries, you may laugh, for you have a worthy heir.

■　■　■

If a little tree grows in the shade of a larger tree, it will die small.

■　■　■

An intelligent enemy is better than a stupid friend.

■　■　■

Don't try to make someone hate the person he loves, for he will still go on loving, but he will hate you.

■　■　■

It is better to be loved than feared.

A paddle here, a paddle there,—the canoe stays still.

■ ■ ■

However full the house, the hen finds a corner to lay in.

■ ■ ■

Only a monkey understands a monkey.

■ ■ ■

If you climb up a tree, you must climb down the same tree.

■ ■ ■

A big fish is caught with big bait.

■ ■ ■

He who refuses a gift will not fill his barn.

53

Quarrels end, but words once spoken never die.

■   ■   ■

If a single hair has fallen from your head, you are not yet bald.

■   ■   ■

He who upsets a thing should know how to rearrange it.

■   ■   ■

A cow must graze where she is tied.

■   ■   ■

An orange never bears a lime.

■   ■   ■

Invite some people into your parlor, and they will come into your bedroom.

■   ■   ■

The sweet rice is eaten quickly.

■   ■   ■

An elephant's head is no load for a child.

54

Do not tell the man who is carrying you that he stinks.

■   ■   ■

It is the wandering dog that finds the old bone.

■   ■   ■

To try and to fail, is not laziness.

In the ocean, one does not need to sow water.

■   ■   ■

He who does not shave you, does not cut you.

■   ■   ■

A thief is always under suspicion.

To be without a friend, is to be poor, indeed.

. . .

A coward is full of precaution.

. . .

Poverty is slavery.

. . .

Wisdom does not come overnight.

. . .

Do not walk into a snake-pit with your eyes open.

. . .

Water and milk do not mix.

. . .

One cannot count on riches.

. . .

A brother is like one's shoulder.

. . .

Where I make a living, there is my home.

56

A termite can do nothing to a stone save lick it.

▪ ▪ ▪

A little shrub may grow into a tree.

▪ ▪ ▪

Let rats shoot arrows at each other.

Do not mend your neighbor's fence before looking to your own.

57

A sheep cannot bleat in two different places at the same time.

■   ■   ■

Events follow one another like the days of the week.

■   ■   ■

Even the night has ears.

■   ■   ■

Everything has an end.

■   ■   ■

We start as fools and become wise through experience.

■   ■   ■

Even flies have ears.

■   ■   ■

Do not make a dress for the baby before the child is born.

■   ■   ■

In the world all things are two and two.

A roaring lion kills no game.

■ ■ ■

Only a fool tries to jump fire.

■ ■ ■

With wealth one wins a woman.

Do not leave your host's house, throwing mud in his well.

■ ■ ■

A word uttered cannot be taken back.

When the man is away, the monkey eats up the maize and enters the hut.

■   ■   ■

A half loaf is better than no bread.

■   ■   ■

Do not call to a dog with a whip in your hand.

■   ■   ■

The horse who arrives early gets good drinking water.

■   ■   ■

A fault confessed is half redressed.

■   ■   ■

One does not cross a river without getting wet.

■   ■   ■

Darkness conceals the hippopotamus.

■   ■   ■

A horse has four legs, yet it often falls.

The most beautiful fig may contain a worm.

■　■　■

Without life, there is nothing.

■　■　■

Follow the customs or flee the country.

■　■　■

The rich are always complaining.

■　■　■

Even an ant may harm an elephant.

■　■　■

Copying everybody else all the time, the monkey one day cut his throat.